THE LEPRECHAUN'S STORY

by Richard Kennedy • illustrated by Marcia Sewall

A Unicorn Book   E. P. Dutton   New York

Library of Congress Cataloging in Publication Data
Kennedy, Richard.   The leprechaun's story.
(A Unicorn book)

SUMMARY: A tradesman meets a leprechaun and is determined
that he won't be tricked out of a pot of gold.
[1. Leprechauns—Fiction]   I. Sewall, Marcia.   II. Title.
PZ7.K385Le   1979   [E]   79-11410   ISBN: 0-525-33472-6

Published in the United States by E. P. Dutton, a Division
of Elsevier-Dutton Publishing Company, Inc., New York

Published simultaneously in Canada by Clarke,
Irwin & Company Limited, Toronto and Vancouver

Editor: Emilie McLeod

Printed in the U.S.A.   First Edition 10 9 8 7 6 5 4 3 2 1

For the O'Keefes

In fair Ireland there came along a country road a village tradesman, strolling at his ease and looking about to see what profit might come of it. He poked his cane about himself, thinking all the while how generous and lovely the world was to a fellow who was quick with his wits.

Presently he was walking alongside a hedgerow, and he heard a soft humming from the other side. So with care not to make a sound, he parted the branches to see the matter of it. And right there was sitting a leprechaun busy at making a pair of small soft boots, for leprechauns are cobblers to fairies, as you might know.

"Arrah!" cries the tradesman with a great shout, jumping through the hedge. "There ye be, ye little imp, and my eyes are right on ye till ye take me to the gold treasure!"

For that's the way it is if you come upon a leprechaun. If you keep your eyes on him and not close them or look away, then he must take you to a gold treasure. But the leprechaun will try to trick you into looking away.

So the leprechaun looks up and says, "Faith, and it's the truth, I must take ye to the gold. But ye'll have no use for gold if ye don't look out for that tree that's about to fall on yerself."

"Bad luck to ye, leprechaun," says the tradesman. "D'ye think ye'll be tricking me so easy?" And he did not look around for any falling tree, but kept his eyes on the little man.

"Ye may be clever," says the leprechaun, "but not clever enough to keep that tiger from leaping on yer back."

"Och! and that's a feeble trick," says the tradesman. "There be no tigers in Ireland." And he did not look about for any tiger, but kept his eyes steadily on the leprechaun.

The little man glanced down the road. "Ah, and there's a glorious sight!" says he. "A prancing white horse and a bonny lass riding with her skirts blowing in the breeze."

"Ye come closer that time," says the tradesman. "Sure, and there are beauties in Ireland, but I'll not be looking at this one. Me eyes are right on ye."

"That they are," says the leprechaun. "Another stitch at my work and it's off to the gold with us." He put his attention to his work for a few moments as the tradesman watched him, and with a final snip he was done with the boots. "There!" says the leprechaun and stands up.

But on that moment he jumps backward and cries out. "God's mercy! The devil himself has popped up behind ye!"

"Aye?" says the tradesman. "And he may have reason. But away with yer tricks, me little darling. I haven't blinked me eyes since first spying ye, and now it's off to the gold with us."

"Sure, and there's no fooling ye this day," sighs the leprechaun, tucking his needles in his belt. "Aye, it's off to the gold. Do ye be ready for the journey?"

"Ready as yerself," says the tradesman. "And please yer tinyness, just walk in front where I can keep me eyes on ye."

So off they went—not on the roadway, but across the lovely green countryside.

Soon they came upon a rope bridge stretched over a small river, and the leprechaun crossed first, very carefully. As the tradesman was crossing the swinging bridge the leprechaun says, "Watch yer feet or ye'll be falling." But the tradesman crossed safely without taking his eyes off the little man.

A shallow lake stood in their way a short distance onward, and a flat-bottomed skiff was pulled upon the shore. Boarding it, the leprechaun handed the tradesman a pole and took one himself; then they proceeded to push themselves across the lake. In the center of the lake the skiff tipped dangerously to one side. The leprechaun cries out, "Look to yer pole or we'll go over!" But the tradesman stared at the leprechaun and the boat righted itself and they landed safely on the farther shore.

They came next to a small canyon. A rope was fastened to a high tree branch on which they could swing across. The leprechaun did so and landed lightly on the other side. He swung the rope back to the tradesman, who then pushed off from his side. "Watch the ground when ye drop off or ye'll be breaking a leg!" cries the leprechaun, but the tradesman keeps his eyes right on the little man and lands safely after all.

The last difficulty was a high cliff in their way. It was a dangerous ascent, and the leprechaun climbed slowly and carefully. When he was at the top, the tradesman began his climb. Many times the leprechaun called down to him to watch his hands and mind his feet, and to be careful for this and that loose rock, and to give him good advice regarding broken necks and cracked skulls. But still the tradesman would not take his eyes off the leprechaun, and finally he made it safely to the top. There they sat down and rested.

"Whew!" says the leprechaun. "Ye be a greedy man to go along so blindly in those dangers."

"Call it what ye will," says the tradesman. "And now for the gold, according to the rules."

"Aye," says the leprechaun, "and ye deserve it, the whole pot of gold. Yet it's very sad I am for the woman."

"What woman is that ye speak of?"

"The poor woman I was thinking to give

the gold to before ye discovered me. So needy she is, and such a fine soul."

"Truth, and many people are poor," says the tradesman.

"Truth indeed," says the leprechaun, "but for this poor woman it's been just one mis- fortune against another. Close yer eyes and picture how it is with her while I tell ye the story of it."

"It's very well I can picture the story with me eyes open and looking right at ye."

"As ye say," says the leprechaun. "Well, she lives in a hut that's no more than a patch on the ground, and she has five children. Her husband was made blind when he was kicked in the head by the horse."

"Ah, that's a shame," says the tradesman. "But it's lucky he is to be alive, and a horse is always valuable."

"That it is, but the horse broke his leg when he kicked the man and had to be put out of his pain, ye know. Then the man went to walking into a well, and it was through for him in this world."

"But sure the poor family was left with a cow at least?" asks the tradesman.

"Faith, and ye might call it a cow," says the leprechaun. "It gave no milk and couldn't be turned with a switch or the name of any saint. The quare heathen beast wandered into the forest and was lost, but not until she attended to trampling the garden down."

"So the poor family hasn't a garden even?"

"It's grubs and roots for them now," says the leprechaun, "and sore hungry the children are. The oldest is only eight. None have shoes, and the baby hasn't any clothes at all."

"Pitiful," says the tradesman, taking a handkerchief out and touching the corner of his eye. "I was a poor lad meself."

"Then ye have the heart to understand. The baby crawls on the filthy floor when the poor woman is out digging grubs, and it's terrible the way the rats go at him, and the other children just sit about crying from hunger."

"But sure they have a dog to catch the rats?"

"They have, but he's got only three legs and is no use for it."

"God's toes, it's a sad story," says the tradesman, blowing and wiping his nose.

"Is yer own dear mother alive?" asks the leprechaun.

"No, and God rest her soul."

"Aye, it's like yer own sainted mother this woman is," says the leprechaun. "The children are starving away before her eyes, sick most often now in want of money for a doctor to attend their fevers."

The tradesman began to weep softly.

"And think of it," says the leprechaun. "Yer own self will soon have a whole pot of gold."

The tradesman sniffled. "Aye, 'tis a strange world indeed."

The leprechaun nodded. "And them so needy for only a single gold piece."

"Aye," said the tradesman, blowing his nose. "There's no understanding it."

"Now it's all yer own fair winnings," says the leprechaun. "Yet there's a favor I'd be asking ye."

"And what is that?" sobs the tradesman.

"So very little they have," says the leprechaun. "And the poor woman is so weak she can't raise the axe to chop wood. Last of all they sold their cooking pot. Now the children must eat their grubs raw and cold."

"Och, the poor woman, the poor children!" the tradesman sobs out.

"For the favor then," says the leprechaun. "D'ye suppose that when ye take the gold ye could leave the pot for the poor family to cook their grubs in?"

"God's name!" bawled the tradesman. "It's the saddest story I've ever heard. Merciful heaven, let's leave them the pot!"

And he was so overcome by the plight of the poor family and his own charity that he began to weep in fullness, and he buried his face in his hands and shook with sobbing.

A few moments later when he looked up, the leprechaun was gone. Then the tradesman realized that the little man had made up the story. There was no poor woman, no hungry children, no rats and no three-legged dog. It was all a trick to make him cry and look away from the leprechaun. So the tradesman put his face into his handkerchief again and bawled more than ever before.